ON THE ROAD TO DAMASCUS

WRITTEN BY
NANCY FULLWOOD

1936
BRADFORD PUBLISHING COMPANY
NEW YORK

Copyright 1931
By NANCY FULLWOOD

All rights reserved. This book, or parts thereof, may not be reproduced in any form without permission of the author.

First Printing, 1935
Second Printing, 1936

PRINTED IN THE UNITED STATES OF AMERICA
BY THE BRADFORD PRESS, INC., NEW YORK

" . . . and knew that beyond the rapture of things seen with the eye was the throbbing world of things not seen but known, of things not held but felt, of things not measured in surety but treasured in hope. With love coming to one and all with each new day as wind and light come, the heavens were opened and the world stood disclosed in a new beauty. To the enchantment had come music.

Fiona Macleod

ON THE ROAD TO DAMASCUS
By
николи Nancy Fullwood

*E*VERY MAN IS DESTINED TO TREAD THE ROAD TO DAMASCUS, which may be interpreted as the road to spiritual illumination.

A great host of people today have placed their feet on this road. Some of them are aware of what is ahead and others are stumbling blindly over the bare, sharp stones which lie where the road begins. It is no easy journey upon which man must, sooner or later, embark. It requires courage, determination and discrimination. But the reward is great.

Many people have asked me to write the story of my own journey along the ever-widening road to illumination. Not that I have reached the goal by any means, but my face is turned that way and I am walking with many toward the light of understanding.

I have not been inclined to write my story before because of the unusual nature of some of the experiences I have had. I do not consider phenomena, as such, important, but when they prove themselves prophetic and true, that is another matter. So, because of the great number of people who have wanted to know about the beginning and development of what they call my "super-natural" experiences, I will start at the very beginning and write of the time when I was first told that I had an impressionable gift of some sort.

In the year 1903 I was visiting in Norfolk, Virginia, and a friend invited me to attend a seance with her. My first impulse was to decline. I had never thought of going to anything of the kind and if I had I should have dismissed it from my mind as a thing to be avoided by sane people. My friend laughed at me and finally persuaded me to go. I went with many misgivings. You see, I was reared in a Scotch Presbyterian environment. My grandfather was a Presbyterian minister and there were several ministers of that faith in my family when I was a girl. Years later some one said that my environment was a perfect one for the strange and beautiful experiences which were to be mine, for the Scotch are a mystical, canny people and while I was never particularly pious, yet I had this mystical, devotional quality in my blood. This probably did have much to do with the kind of development I underwent. Be that as it may. In that year of 1903, doors opened for me into a hitherto unheard of realm of life which seemed as natural to me as the world of everyday. I was not a student of mysticism, philosophy or occultism. I had never heard of what is called "the Mysteries". I didn't know there were any. I had never read a book on these subjects, nor did I know one person who knew any more than I did about such things. I was grown and married and the mother of two little sons before I became conscious of vital, though invisible influences in my life. The first intimation of this came from the medium who conducted the seance I attended with my friend. The medium's name was Madam Newman. An ardent group of believers sat on either side of her around a large table. I was self-conscious and silent. I longed to ask a question but couldn't get a sound from my lips. She paid no attention to me until toward the end of the evening when she leaned over the table and spoke directly to me. "Do you know you are inspirational?" she asked. It was all so new to me. I didn't know what she meant and said so.

"Learn to be still and you will know," was her wise reply. I was somewhat bewildered and not in the least a still person, so I answered, "I am afraid the order is too big for me. I have never been still. Something about me is always moving." She smiled at me patiently and instead of answering my doubt, she said: "Sit at the piano at dusk and play. Don't think about what you are playing. Just play on. I think you will be surprised at what you do."

I was only mildly interested and not at all impressed with her suggestion as to my musical ability. Besides, I had two babies at that time and had other music to listen to at dusk. So I didn't obey. I didn't know then that life operates through seemingly casual contacts and that it is our part to be alert in every way that we may not miss an experience which may prove to be the key to a door through which new vistas may stretch out before us. Such a key did this stranger prove to be for me, although it was not apparent to me at the time.

Later that same year I was in Atlanta,

Georgia, where I met an old gentleman from Texas. The meeting was apparently quite accidental. I don't even remember his name, but during the short time I was in his company he came up to me and said in a low voice, "Do you know you are inspirational?" To say that I was amazed is putting it mildly. I told him that I had heard that before and asked him what he meant by it.

"Write," he said. "Keep a pencil and paper near you all the time. Just write at random, paying no attention to what you are writing and don't read it for a month. I think you will be surprised at what you write." The very words the woman in Norfolk had used.

It was an interesting coincidence, I thought, that two strangers so many miles apart should have told me the same thing about myself, of whom they knew nothing. But I didn't take it seriously. It seemed rather amusing to me and I used to tell it to my friends hoping to impress them, but I didn't know what I was talking about and they didn't either, so my little scheme didn't work and I dismissed the matter from my mind.

Then a man named Allen Connett came to Atlanta, lecturing on what he called Practical Psychology. Optimism, it might have been called as I remember it. I attended the lecture and after it was over, to my surprise the speaker stepped down from the platform and asked me to remain, saying that he wished to speak to me. I did so and he asked me earnestly what it was I wanted to do. It was an astonishing question from a total stranger. I told him I had never thought of doing anything other than being a busy wife and mother. He looked at me steadily and announced: "You have something to do and I should be happy to help you learn to be still and listen."

There it was again! What could it

mean and whatever it was, how could these people know it? I began to have quite an opinion of myself. I hadn't the remotest idea why. Friends who knew me well looked at me more carefully, hoping for the best, but were compelled to acknowledge that they saw nothing in me to get excited about, especially as they knew I would never be still. But this psychologist didn't lose faith in me. He seemed positively to know that I was in tune with invisible forces and had to do something about it. The idea was intriguing and although I didn't understand, I was willing to be shown. Dr. Connett taught me to be still, that is, to get my little personal, assertive mind out of the way, and to allow a deeper phase of myself to come forth. I found that this deeper self is like a radio station in tune with the universe, and that it was quite simple for me to relax and drop the hectic, outer mental consciousness and slip into the realm of forces known through feeling and intuition.

Being still within, I learned, is the same as being still without, only deeper.

I wonder where this good friend, Dr. Connett, is today. I am sure he would be interested to know how this latent thing he sensed in me has developed and expanded like the widening ripples in a lake which start with the simple dropping of a pebble in its waters.

As soon as I learned the art of being still within, things began to happen. It was like a new and fascinating game to me. I know now that many people have had like experiences, but at that time I knew nothing about it. There seemed to be two of me. One sat there and watched the other one walk along strange streets and look into strange faces. I heard bands playing and beautiful voices singing. There was music everywhere. I recalled the woman in Norfolk who in some subtle way connected me with music. At first Dr. Connett was my only audience. He was almost as excited as I was when I described things I saw with my eyes closed, things far more amazing than anything I had ever seen with them open. I was always completely conscious at these times and have never been entranced in my life.

Once I was sitting very still listening within. I sank into a soft black substance. It seemed very deep. In this blackness there appeared a row of lighted footlights outlining an invisible stage. Then out of this blackness came a white cloud. It glowed like phosphorus and kept coming closer and getting clearer until it took form and I saw that it was a woman. She seemed to be hanging there in deep black space. I gazed at her breathlessly, afraid to move lest she slip back into that invisible realm from which she had come. As I wondered what she was going to do, a piano and a young man appeared and I knew she was going to sing. Then the floor of the stage came out like a photograph developing in a dark room and the complete picture of a woman standing on a stage about to sing, stood out sharply. I saw her accompanist sit down before the piano and play, and I saw that she was singing, but I couldn't hear a sound, though I waited until it all melted into the blackness. I determined to try again hoping that she would come back. Imagine my delight when, a few days later she returned in the same setting. There she stood smiling at me. This time I heard her lovely voice as she sang a plaintive, minor melody that had an overtone which I felt must permeate the universe, but I couldn't hear the words of the song. It ended with a humming sound of M-m-m-m-m, long drawn out. Its effect on me was like the raising of a violin string to the breaking point. My heart beat like a triphammer. The third time she came I heard and learned both the words and the melody. After that she came often and not always alone. Sometimes she brought a youth with a high, clear soprano voice, and sometimes a man with a rich baritone. At other times she accompanied herself on a harp. I have many songs I learned from these materially invisible singers. I was not a trained musician and it has always been difficult for me to memorize a song, but these songs seemed to be a part of me. I could write them down long after I heard them.

Then other friends heard about this interesting game—for it seemed just that to me—which Dr. Connett and I were playing. They wished to join us. So we formed a group of men and women who met every week that winter in Atlanta and tried out all sorts of tests in clairvoyance, telepathy, psychometry, etc. I was not familiar with these names at that time, and not until years later did I know that these performances were well known in others who, for the most part operated under trance conditions, and didn't remember what they had seen or heard when they awakened.

The way we made these tests was

simple and effective. Our friends in different parts of the city would note what they were doing at the time when the members of our group were sitting together. I would sit there and see my other self go into their houses and see what they were doing, hear their dogs barking, etc., and report. Then later these friends would call us on the telephone and report their actions so that we could check up on me. I was invariably right. I seemed to be perfectly en rapport with everything to which I turned my attention. I began to get a sense of the oneness of life.

I had an example of that powerful, all-pervading invisible influence which we call the Christmas Spirit. A few days before Christmas a cantata was enacted before my inner vision. It was called the HOLY STAR. I told the story of this musical play as it unfolded before me, and sang the solos with the leading lady, who was the same singer I first heard. There were many children in it. It took two and a half hours to go through it. Unfortunately, the spectators were so absorbed in the phenomenon that no one thought to take it down. The only thing I remember about it is the title and one scene. There was an enormous star high above the left of the stage and the manger scene was in the star. The Three Wise Men stood on the stage with arms upraised to it and sang a beautiful, tender song about the Holy Star.

One of the men who joined our group to the great benefit of all its members, was Robert Bryan Harrison, the widely know and much loved president of The Atlanta Psychological Society. He reported the many interesting tests we made to the Psychical Research Society in New York when Dr. Hyslop, its first president, was alive, and I suppose these reports are reposing somewhere in their archives now.

Having no knowledge of how the invisible forces operate, I was inclined to think that my imagination played an important part in my experiences, although it was a mystery to me why I hadn't known before that I had such an imagination.

Then, at Mr. Harrison's suggestion, we made a test which proved to me that it was not imagination, at least not as I had thought of it. Today, I know that little, if anything, is known about true imagination, in spite of the many theories set forth. I have a theory, yes, but as this story is a straight narrative of experiences with invisible forces, I cannot go into that now.

Mr. Harrison suggested that I send my other self to visit his brother who lived in a distant city and report what he was doing at four o'clock one Saturday afternoon. He wrote his brother and asked him to note what he was doing, then write us, agreeing to write him what I said he was doing. We arranged it so that the letters would cross and there would be no chance for influence or suggestion. The brother agreed to help with the test. Up to this time I had accepted all this like a child with an interesting toy—a fairy tale for which one has no explanation.

I sat there with our group on the appointed afternoon. We talked it over a bit, then in an instant I was in the town where Mr. Harrison's brother lived, but in that instant I went through every move I would have made had I been making the trip in the ordinary, physical manner. I went to the station, bought my ticket, got on the train and arrived at my destination. I got off the train and into a bus. and had a distinct feeling of annoyance because a very fat man wouldn't move over and let me sit down. My friends laughed when I told them, but the poor fat man, how could he know that an invisible woman was pushing in beside him. The bus went up a wide street and I described a house on the right with a profusion of flowers in the yard. As I described it one of the women with us recognized it as her mother's home. Later, the bus stopped before a red brick Courthouse in the center of a large lawn. I knew, in some strange, inner way, that I was going to get out there.

I went in the Courthouse and passed through room after room, describing the men in them. Then I entered an office where there was a man standing by a window, looking out.

"I have found your brother," I announced to Mr. Harrison. "His figure is like yours."

"Ask him his name," he suggested.

"John," I replied, which was correct.

"What is he doing?"

I saw myself standing there before Mr. Harrison's brother, seeing everything clearly, so I answered: "He is standing by a window watching two boys fighting on the lawn."

Then we wrote a letter to this man and told him what I had seen. The following afternoon his letter came in which he said that at four o'clock he was standing by the window in his office watching two negro boys tussle for sugar cane. To our surprise he said that he saw me, that I stood before him as plainly as he had ever seen anything. He said he would know me anywhere and described me minutely, even the color of my eyes and the clothes I wore. I knew then that I had not merely imagined the experience.

Unfortunately, I never saw this man in the flesh. It would have been more than interesting if he had been able to recognize me in a crowd of people. However, this incident was a milestone on the road along which I was destined to go, although I didn't realize this at that time.

After the unbelievable experiences of

that winter I found that I was greatly depleted. I became pale and thin and nervously exhausted. Not one of our group, least of all myself, knew that we had been drawing on a subtle nerve essence in my body which was needed for what we know as normal functioning, but I knew I must stop that sort of thing. Consternation reigned when I announced to my friends that I was through. They said it was blasphemous to give up such a gift as mine. But this "gift" was a sort of a dream to me and was not as important as my health, my home and my children. So I was adamant. I shut the door into that realm of the invisible forces. In the light of what has taken place since that year, I look upon that phase of my experiences as a preparation for those which followed long afterward.

We moved from Atlanta to Birmingham, Alabama. In 1907 we bought a place in the country, about four miles from the city, and went there to live. I lived a wholesome, out-of-door life, raising boys and chickens. My health was entirely restored. I had no return of phenomena of any kind in my life. No book or person came my way to explain the unusual experiences I had had.

Five years passed. Then right out of the blue strange things began to happen to me. One night I was awakened by a terrific wind. I sat up in bed and literally had to hold the cover about me to keep it from being blown from the bed. I thought there was a hurricane and expected the roof of our bungalow to go off any minute. At last I got up and staggered in the wind to close the window on the other side of the room, but when I raised my arms to lower the sash, I realized that there was no wind. It was a calm, full moon night. Not a breath of air stirring. I could hear the trees breathing, it was so still.

Later that same summer I was awakened by fire. I sprang up, wide awake. The whole room was in a glow, and all around, just below the picture molding, were tongues of flame about ten inches long. They were about a foot apart and might have been painted there like a border, except that they were leaping. On the wall was an enormous bow-knot of fire, throbbing like living coals. There are no words to describe the stillness about me. It was like being in a vacuum where there was no living thing but the fire and myself, and I melted into the fire and was one with it. After what seemed ages, it faded out, and I got up and went all over the house, feeling certain that something must be burning. But everything was all right; a great calmness everywhere.

I knew nothing of symbolism so I had no explanation of these phenomenal experiences. But I met a man in Birmingham who was a student of such things. He knew of the experiences I had had in Atlanta years before and was expecting a different phase to appear. He approved of my having given it up and closed that door, as it were. Because of that, he was certain of something, he never told me what. He interpreted these experiences for me. He said that in the sacred books there were many accounts of symbolic visions and that their history had come down through the ages recording certain results which followed, so they had come to have definite meanings.

The wind, he said, meant a revelation —that I was going to have something revealed to me. The tongues of flame, he said, meant the coming of a child or a new birth, and the bow-knot of fire meant a religious upheaval. That was twenty-two years ago in the woods of Alabama, and there was no apparent sign of any upheaval in my world. But today it seems to me that those prophesies have been fulfilled. This man told me that in his opinion the sensation of the wind was all in my own body, that every atom of it was being quickened or keyed up, as it were, preparatory to greater phenomena than I had known.

Five years passed again with nothing unusual in my life; 1917 came, and I had a recurrence of the sensitiveness I had experienced in Atlanta. I was continually reading the minds of my family and could report just what my boys had done at different times during the day in the city. It was a source of interest and amusement. A different phase of the experiences began. I received many messages from invisible communicants giving me advice. Some of these announced themselves as spirits of the so-called dead. They would give me their names and tell me where to find their people. I tried in every way to follow their directions, but to no avail.

For weeks I carried this on with deep interest and high hope. Then I heard a call. I designate it as a call, but I do not mean a physical sound. It is an inner hearing, but it is none the less clear and unmistakable. Intuitive hearing, is perhaps a better name for it. I knew this was something entirely different because of the change in my feeling. There was a quickened sensation, accompanied by ecstasy. I wrote this call—"Hear me: *Sano Tarot.*" I wrote it as one word, "Sanotarot"—and thought it was an attempt to spell sanitary. My son, Harry, said: "Mother, your friend is a poor speller, but he's clean. He won't say a word until he has announced that he is sanitary." That was quite a joke in the family. It was more than a year before I learned that TAROT stood by itself as a word, or symbol, and that it meant the Law, the law of equilibrium on which creation is based.

It seemed astonishing to me that I should be writing on such a subject, since I knew nothing about it. But I soon found that this was something not to be denied. Day and night I wrote. I didn't know what the writing meant, but it caught me up in its rhythm and not only filled me with ecstasy, but the ecstasy communicated itself to others who were with me at times. I had two dear friends, Josephine Brooks and Deborah Lewis, and I wish to express my appreciation for their sympathetic understanding and love. Those were happy and absorbing times.

The writing brought the feeling of a presence which was so real and definite that I began to talk to it.

"Who are you?" I asked.

"I am he who sits at the head of the table in the Hermitage, where the life Forces center and from which they radiate to the far corners of the universe, which is the temple not made with hands," was the answer.

This didn't tell me much, but I knew it was one in authority speaking because of the statement: "I am he who sits at the head of the table."

I continued to write as the presence went on: "You have been ordained, not because of favor, but because of a balanced channel of physical and spiritual forces, to record a right royal song singing of the rose tree on the road to the spring of life. There is a garden of roses in the temple grounds. In this garden there stands a tree, singing to right royal Hierophants. Love is the rose tree's fruit. It smells of rich, ripe wheat in harvest time. It showers its wealth on you in Inspiration."

I felt a great harmony and uplift in these words spoken by *Sano Tarot* but I didn't know what the strange statement meant. Then these words were added: "The spirit of *Sano Tarot* is the spirit of Inspiration and peace is the reward of him who has received the Insignia of Seers."

It was an entirely new language to me. I knew of course, that it was symbolic, but being able to interpret symbolic meanings was another matter. I sensed its beauty and truth, but it was years before I really knew the meaning of this statement.

I asked *Sano Tarot* why I was being given this matter. "Why don't you give it to someone who knows what you are talking about?" I asked.

The answer to this was: "That you do not know is the very reason why I can give it to you. Your mind is like an open, sunlit field. There is no shadow on it." I took this to mean that I was not cluttered up with opinions, theories, dogmas and creeds.

I used to laugh a great deal. It was all so joyous and beautiful. Then I felt that perhaps I should be more serious and dignified, so I asked if it was all right for me to laugh. I received the happy response: "Yes, laugh! The gods are laughing with you. It is your very joy that has opened the temple gates."

So I wrote on and on.

As the writing progressed I realized that I was being given a story of creation. Familiar Biblical names were signed to many of the communications. It occurred to me that these names were symbols or forms, through which the invisible forces were manifesting themselves to me. I first discovered that there was a difference between them by the change in my feeling as I transcribed the different phases of the story. Each of them tells the same story from a slightly different angle. I felt as if I were in some strange inner school. Things that had seemed obscure to me, or to which I had given no thought at all, suddenly stood out clearly and simply.

Presbyterianly speaking, it was a source of amazement when these invisible beings spoke of themselves as "the gods."

Something in me accepted the truth of their existence, though I had no understanding whatever of what they might be. Then, as usual, *Sano Tarot* knew my wonder and uncertainty and explained the gods to me. "The gods," he said, "in no sense interfere with the Nameless One whom the people have called God. The symbol 'god' in the cipher code of vibration means a ruler or creative center of a given expression of the life Forces. The primal gods are seven in number. They have been likened to the seven Spirits before the throne. They are the creative centers of the seven primal Forces which cross themselves in the lowered vibration of earth, seeking balance one with the other, thus bringing the kingdom of harmony into earth."

During that year Deborah Lewis visited New York and someone gave her a copy of a magazine called THE WORD. In it there was an article entitled THE SECRET DOCTRINE OF THE TAROT, by Paul

F. Case. Imagine the delight of finding someone who could enlighten me from another viewpoint on the subject about which I was writing. I wrote to Mr. Case at once and told him that I was writing a document on the Tarot, and asked him to tell me something about it. He was interested and very kind. He gave me much information from his splendid store of knowledge of the ancient Tarot. In one of his letters to me he said that I had received a direct revelation—it was certainly a revelation to me.

During the years I have learned more and more. I have learned that a very, very old exposition of the fundamental Law of Equilibrium is set forth in a pack of seventy-eight cards called the Tarot cards. These cards are decorated with symbolic pictures, numbers and signs for him to decipher who can. I feel that this interpretation of the Law is an intellectual one, while the one given to me is the essence or spiritual interpretation.

These ancient Tarot cards are ancestors of our modern playing cards. Both packs are arranged in four suits which symbolize the four basic elements, Earth, Air, Fire and Water, which correspond to Body, Mind, Spirit and Soul in human life. I think this truth is profoundly significant for in it we find the same Law operating yesterday, today and forever.

As the writing progressed I became deeply interested in *Sano Tarot's* exposition of the law of polarity. I learned that sex means much more than the physical union of men and women. Sex is the universal law of creation and every relationship on every plane is a marriage of forces, either harmonious or discordant, according to the harmony of the forces fused. Life is a cosmic marriage song. All the eternal pairs of opposites—the sun and the moon, light and dark, the currents of air, the strata of the soil, the intellect and the intuition, man and woman —are seeking balance that creation may express.

The writings were full of repetitions which were presented with a rhythm which seemed to me to beat like a drum. In my ignorance I asked if I might cut out the repetitions and condense the writings. *Sano Tarot* said: "No. Leave the matter as you have recorded it. Rhythmic repetition is my method of expanding and building the brain cells of my people." And little by little 1 began to experience the magic of expanding consciousness.

Two years of intensive seeking for light coupled with genuine amusement began when this instruction was given to me: "Place a terrapin on your middle and you can see me and hear my voice."

What an astonishing order, but what could be more wonderful than to see and speak to the gods face to face! I was not enthusiastic about the method suggested, but I have always obeyed the orders which have come from what I considered celestial spheres. I would have wrapped myself up in snakes if the order had been such, but I did resist a bit. "Must it be on my middle?" I asked. "Can't I place it on someone else's middle and watch it work?"

But no, that wouldn't do. It must be on my own middle. So I agreed: "All right. But where will I get a terrapin?"

The answer was: "Sit very still and I will place a terrapin on your middle and you can see me and hear my voice."

If I had known anything about the language of symbols perhaps I might have been more intelligent, but knowing nothing, I took it all literally. I grasped the arms of the chair, thrust my middle out as far as I could and waited. I would not have been surprised if a terrapin had materialized out of nowhere and dropped on my middle with a thud. But nothing happened although I sat there patiently for a long time. Then I laughed at myself and went to bed.

This was in 1918. Just then the gods brought another loved and helpful friend into my life, Rosa Julian. She invited me to spend a week-end with her in her country home in northern Alabama. Deborah Lewis and Josephine Brooks were also invited. That visit was the first time I had been away from my home in years. I was the kind of woman who felt that without her presence in the home everything would go to ruin. I thought that without me my boys would wander away and get into trouble, and the chickens would die. But to my own astonishment and that of my family, I accepted this invitation, thereby reversing my mother complex. I had a sneaking conviction that my family was secretly delighted to be left alone for a few days.

I shall never forget the beauty of that place in the foothills of the Blue Ridge Mountains. It looked like the Promised Land to me. It was the second week in May, 1918. A book could be written about that visit and our experiences there. It was like a great spiritual convention. I was exceedingly alive and receptive. Ethereal forms moved about under those great oak trees—Cherokee Chiefs, and ancient Egyptian priests dressed in priestly robes and insignia. They spoke about the beginning of a new cycle of time when the veil between the visible and invisible worlds would disappear, and we would know that there is no death. We were given Sun rituals and taught how to use them. I know it all sounds unbelievable. I would not have believed it myself if I had not seen and heard things that I could never have imagined.

Sano Tarot told me that I was there by his order, which explained my unusual willingness to leave home. I was given another symbolic message which I took literally. *Sano Tarot* said: "On the branch of the tree by the spring is a nest of eggs. When the eggs mature and the birds are on the wing, my Force, Inspiration, will permeate the dark planet Earth."

With high hope that something was going to be revealed to me, I went out and wandered about the woods. I found a tree which seemed to stand as a sentinel over a clear, bubbling spring which overflowed and formed a little stream and disappeared under the thick pine needles on the ground. But alas! there was no nest of eggs in the tree. I was a bit discouraged but *Sano Tarot* knew that I had at least tried to understand and I suppose I should have been comforted when he said: "As you journey on the road to Damascus the light of the ages will make plain the way." But that seemed a long time to wait for an explanation of the strange symbolic statement, for it was not likely that I would ever go to Damascus. Years later I met one who knew and he told me that such symbolic speech has to do with states of consciousness in man. He said it was necessary to teach man in symbols because he could not bear the full light of his own spiritual nature. It was then that I learned that the statement "on the road to

Damascus" meant on the road to spiritual illumination, and on this road the light of ever-increasing awareness does indeed make plain the way. In the Bible there is the story of Saul's illumination on the road to Damascus*, and from this more light was given to me.

*Acts 9, 3 to 10.

I told my three friends that the next thing we had to do was to place a terrapin on our middles. There was a moment of silent amazement, then, with great merriment, they all agreed to follow the order. Our hostess offered her young son a dollar if he would find a terrapin for us.

Then we decided to walk in the woods and search for one ourselves. We planned to take turns in placing it on our middles and see what would happen. It was great fun. Josephine Brooks is gifted with very sensitive and clear intuition, and the truth came to her first. In the midst of our laughter and wonder she exclaimed: "Stop! That doesn't mean a live terrapin. It is a symbol and means concentration."

Then we sat down under a great oak tree and *Sano Tarot* spoke to us through me. He must have been amused, if the gods know amusement, and I know they do, for humor is one of the attributes of spiritual understanding.

The explanation given to us that day was that the terrapin was used as a symbol of the balanced concentration, because, like the solar plexus, which is the foundation of life in the physical body, it draws its life forces together in one center ("under one shell") and balances its movements through instinct. From the solar plexus, the seven life Forces expand like the petals of the lotus and express themselves in our lives as principles. He likened the solar plexus to the Mother of Life in the human body. Here, in this center, the life Forces lie dormant until impregnated by the opposite or positive pole, the solar nerve at the navel. He likened this solar center to the seed from which mortals emerge, just as the oak tree springs from the acorn. The foetus forms about the navel or seed, and life enters the body at this point. It thrusts its essence into the solar plexus and from their polarity springs man, the tree of life. The continual throb in the place of their union he called "the sacred heart." Sometimes he speaks of this center of balance as "the ark of the Convenant." "the still place in the altar room of the temple (the body)," "The gate-way where the physical and spiritual Forces are balanced and from which they expand into their full possibilities." He explained that the whole scheme of creation operates in the body.

In an ancient Indian classic I found this: "At the navel, Agni (Fire) sings the seven headed song." This agreed with *Sano Tarot's* statement: "At the navel the seven primal Forces sing together in balance and harmony."

After this experience I began seeking for more light on the subject of the balanced concentration. I accepted *Sano Tarot's* instruction on the subject, but I became obsessed with the desire to know if anyone else had ever heard of this center of balance. For two years I thought I was the only person in the world besides my three friends whom I had told about it, who had ever heard of such a thing. I asked hundreds of people if they knew anything about the navel, and received as many stony stares mingled with disgust. My friends tried to stop me. "Nancy," they would ask, "Can't you think of some topic of conversation besides your navel? It's indecent. It simply isn't done." I was almost ostracized from polite society. *But I had to know.* Then it became a huge joke and my question never failed to bring laughter. No book or person ever came my way to explain it to me until I met Dr.

Tagore, the Indian poet and philosopher. I had a most interesting and satisfying visit with him, and when I asked him my now famous navel question and told him how I had received what illumination I had about it, he looked at me silently, then said: "You have found the key. You must dedicate your life to the One who is speaking through you."

So I continued to follow *Sano Tarot's* teaching with confident joy.

After this, information on the subject began to come to me from many sources. Friends who had laughed at me began to send me quotations they had found in books or heard from teachers, about the importance of the navel center. I was given illuminating books on the subject and discovered that this truth was as old as time, but like most fundamental truths, its significance was lost when man created a mental world for himself, and like the prodigal son, wandered far from home. But today, after aeons of man's self will and the chaos he has created, there are signs that he is once again turning his face toward his Father's house.

During the time I was writing the material now published in the books entitled THE SONG OF SANO TAROT, THE TOWER OF LIGHT and THE LIFE OF ONE WOMAN, I had an experience which may serve to emphasize the necessity of discrimination in contacting the invisible forces. I met a man whom I shall call Mr. "X". He was a teacher of occultism. He gave lectures and taught classes, etc. I had several friends who studied with him and they, being also impressed with my writings, thought it important that I, too, join his classes. But I did not comply with their wishes, and knew very little about him. So imagine my surprise when one day as I was writing I felt a distinct vibratory change which, with me, always means that a different influence is tuning in on my consciousness. I was very curious in those days. It was so amazing, this coming into conscious contact with intelligent, though invisible forces. I had often been cautioned not to allow interference to enter my "channel" which had been "prepared for a given purpose." Maybe I didn't quite understand. Anyway, I listened and received the polite suggestion:

"Mr. 'X' wishes you to call him on the phone." With equal courtesy I asked: "Who are you?" "I am 'X's' slave," was the answer, "I beg you to call my master."

I had never heard the term "slave" used in such a connection and I instinctively knew that it was not constructive, so I said nothing more to it and the invading entity departed without another word. But another day it returned and said: "You must send for 'X'." Then I felt *Sano Tarot's* unmistakable rhythm and received the words: "Do not be deceived. This slave has no right to speak to you. He must die. Bid him go."

"Go!" I commanded.

I was astonished when the slave said: "I cannot go. I am sent by my master 'X' to remain with you until you take your writings to him."

I paid no attention to this and later it came and pleaded: "Pity me. Do not let me die. Send for my master 'X'. With him you will gain wealth and fame."

Not for a moment had I thought of all this as coming from this man "X" until *Sano Tarot* told me that "this slave is an elemental controlled by 'X's' will. 'X' is trying to impress you by his concentrated will and compel you to take the writings to him, for a reason of his own. A desire impelled by a powerful will takes form and fulfills the purpose for which it was created unless it meets an obstacle stronger than itself. Then it loses its power and disintegrates or dies. You do well not to respond to this call."

For weeks this persistent slave was

with me at intervals, but since I paid no attention to it, it finally disappeared. But I learned about the power of the concentrated human will, selfishly used, called "black magic."

When those particular writings were finished, I asked *Sano Tarot* what I must do with the manuscript, if anything. The answer was: "Be still. Do not move until I say move. I am preparing the minds of my people that they may receive my words." So I waited.

I was familiar by this time with the expression "singing" and knew it meant the humming of the vibrating forces within us and all about us. I loved *Sano Tarot's* presentation of life in terms of music. Everything is singing and humming. Each one of us is an orchestra. Every atom is making its own vibratory music and every organ of our body is humming its own tone. He said that the key note of our orchestra sounds in the middle of our body and according to our ability to find our own key note do we have harmony in our music, and so become a part of the great universal orchestra of the spheres. I tried to hear my own vibratory music but I was not very successful. I realized that our physical hearing was too dull to catch the vibratory music of the life forces, but I have discovered that the dullest of us are quick to recognize our likes and dislikes. So we may be said to instinctively sense vibrations, even though we cannot always hear their humming.

That phase of the writings had been finished about a year and a half when *Sano Tarot* told me to journey to "the city singing to upheaval" — the keynote of New York—and to be there on my birthday, June 29th, of that year, 1919. He said: "You will be used as a center of balance in the time of chaos about to fall over that situation."

That was an amazing statement to

me and I didn't know what it meant then but certain experiences have made me somewhat more aware now.

I broke the news gently to my husband that we were going to New York and he broke it to me ungently that we were not going to do any such thing. He said he had no business in New York and woudn't live there if he were given the place. He suggested that I should not get foolish notions into my head, so the matter rested. About two months passed and he had forgotten our little argument. He came in one day quite elated, and asked me how I would like to live in Newark, New Jersey. His business house was going to open a branch there and wanted him to manage it. Well, I saw the invisible hand of destiny operating in my life, but I kept very still about it. So we came to New York and I was in the city on my birthday, just as I was told to be, and I have been here ever since.

In New York I had access to books

and teachers, and for the first time I began to intellectualize what I had written entirely inspirationally. I read and attended lectures and studied this and that interesting theory about life and man's place in it. But I found that the knowledge I had received from invisible sources was more fundamental than anything I heard. I had applied the principle of balance taught me through the years and found that I could say with Walt Whitman:— "Within me latitude widens, longitude lengthens. I contain multitudes."

One of the teachers I met who showed great interest in the writings, thought I had made a mistake in transcribing Timothy's communication about the Four Winds, included in THE SONG OF SANO TAROT. He said that Timothy placed the positions of the basic elements opposite from the positions as given in an authentic diagram he owned. He thought I should change it. I wouldn't do that, but I thought a lot about it and wondered if it were possible that I could have made such a mistake. One morning I was on my way to the telephone to talk over this matter once more with this teacher. All my manuscripts and papers were in another room, so I was surprised to find two sheets of paper lying on the floor beside the telephone table. One lay across the other much as a hand might cover the lower part of a paper directing the reading of the top lines of the under sheet. I leaned over to take the papers from the floor and saw that they contained a message from *Sano Tarot* received some time before. There I read these words: "It is my desire that you change nothing of basic truth in my words. In the story of the Winds, Timothy speaks truth." So that question was settled once and for all. I pinned these sheets of paper together just as I had found them and they are here now on my table, another mute though powerful example of the presence of invisible forces.

By this time my two sons joined us in New York from college. About this time also, I met Claude Bragdon. Those of you who are familiar with his books, or have the good fortune to know him personally, need no word from me as to the great spirit of this man. At once I knew him to be one in authority. I told him about my writings and asked him to read the manuscript and give me his opinion of it. His response was characteristic. He said: "After what you have told me, I wouldn't dare not read it. Much illumination is due to come into the world now from many sources, in this time of transition into a new age. Basic truths will be given to us in new forms, and if there is illumination in only one paragraph of your manuscript, I want it."

I knew this was the attitude of an understanding and spiritual man, and was deeply grateful. After he had read the manuscript, he told me that he considered it important and undoubtedly one of the illuminations of which he had spoken to me. He said that he felt that it was not the time to give it out then but that I would be told when the time came and would be led into the right way to do it. He said that it was a fourth dimensional document. Well, I had never heard of the fourth dimension. I didn't even know there were three. But it became my next task to find out what I could about dimensions, especially the fourth. I pored over Tertium Organum, that epoch making book by P. D. Ouspenski. This book was first published by Claude Bragdon at his own expense, because he considered it a valuable message. That too, was characteristic of this great man. The book was rather difficult for me, since it was intellectual and mathematical—the opposite of my type of mind. But it goes to show that all things work together for one who determinedly demands illumination. I had to concentrate everything in me on that book. Then I began to feel it intuitively. On the night of November 9th,

1923, I was in bed in my room and completely lost in this amazing book. It was about half past ten o'clock when I felt that something had happened in the room. It seemed to be electrified. I felt that someone had come into the room silently. There was a mirror opposite me directly in my line of vision. I looked up quickly and there in the center of the mirror was a pure white, luminous cross with prismatic colors on the ends of the cross piece and on the top, like a colorful knob. I stared at it, scarcely believing my eyes; then I got up and tried to find out what caused it. I am a very practical person and I like to know the cause of things which seem to be unexplainable. I thought this cross was a reflection of some kind. I shook the chandelier and ran my hand over the pictures. I thought if I could cast a shadow over the light of the cross I would know where the reflection came from. But there was no shadow and I couldn't find the cause. Then I turned to get back in bed and there was the cross on the wall beside my bed, directly over my desk. Shimmering white light with rainbow ends. It was so startling that I fell on my knees before it and asked that its meaning be made plain to me. "If this is a sign to me and has to do with the writings, give me a sign that it is a sign. Don't let me fool myself," I implored.

As I rose from my knees there was a report like a pistol shot on the chiffonier, answered by one on a trunk in the far side of the room, which I took for an answer, —"Yes, pay attention."

I couldn't read any more. I kept looking up to see if the cross was still there, and it was. I lay there wondering if anyone else could see it, or if it was one of those things that I see and other people doubt. Then my son, Mebane, came in. As he stepped in the door of my room, he exclaimed: "Hello, what's that? There's a big, white cross on the wall!" Then I knew that he, at least, could see it.

"Yes,'" I answered, "I don't know where it came from. It was not there when I went to bed. You've slept in this room many times and you know it was not here."

"Of course not," he agreed. "Nobody could miss that. I'll find what makes it."

"I hope you can. Go ahead and try," I urged.

He carefully examined everything in the room just as I had done, but could find nothing that might have caused it. He gave it up, saying: "Well, it's got me. I don't know what it is."

We discovered that when he stood in the middle of the room, the cross was in the mirror, on his back and on the wall. The illusion was like an X-ray. It seemed to pass through everything we placed before it, a heavy dictionary, a thick plank —nothing shut it out.

The following morning the cross was still there, and I called Rosa Julian, who was now living in New York, and told her to come out as quickly as she could and see the cross which had appeared in my room.

At once she said, "Why, Nancy, don't you remember the message?"

But I didn't remember any message about a cross, so she said: "Well, I have it here in a note book and I'll come right out and bring it."

She came with the note book in which she had written down many things which had been spoken through my voice, and there was a communication from *Sano Tarot*, received two years before the cross appeared, in which it was said that when in my own development the life Forces had attained certain expansion and balance which corresponded with the balance of the universal life Forces, there would appear before me the sign of the cross. *Sano Tarot* always speaks of the cross as his sign. I understood this somewhat more clearly after he explained the cross that morning. I had never heard of any interpretation of the cross other than the Christian one of a man nailed to a cross to save humanity. *Sano Tarot* said that the cross is the oldest symbol of creation, and that it means the balancing of the positive and negative, or spiritual and physical Forces within us. He said that man is the cross; that each one of us is nailed to his own cross because we have not found perfect balance, and must be held in limitation until we perfect ourselves and lift ourselves from the cross of limitation into the freedom of spirit.

    I thought perhaps the appearance of the cross meant that it was time to do something with the manuscript—have it printed and given out—and I asked if this were true, but the answer was the same: "Be still. Do not move until I say move. Two men will come to assist in the final giving out of my words. One of them is from Egypt.'"

"How will a man from Egypt find me in this great city?" I questioned.

"He will hear of you through the publicity of the cross," came the answer. So I continued to wait.

The cross remained in my room three years. It moved with me twice, once when I changed my room, then my apartment. Many people saw it. I have many affidavits from them, stating that they saw it. But it never had general publicity. It seemed to have a powerful protection about it. Never once did anyone come to see it who was not reverent and deeply impressed. It became a sort of shrine to my friends. Many unutterably beautiful things came to pass before it.

In the message which contained the prophesy of the appearance of the cross, there was also a strange warning: "When my sign appears before you, take your position in the temple for it will be a sign of disaster to the city of your habitation." I had not understood that the reference to the "temple" meant my body and I had never heard the body spoken of as the "city of our habitation", so I thought the familiar prophesy of the destruction of the city of New York was about to be fulfilled. Not until years after the "disaster" began, did one who knew, explain this symbolism to me.

About a year after the cross appeared, I was suddenly taken very ill. I was rushed to the hospital. No one dreamed that I would live. In fact, I didn't. I died. I know I died, but they brought me back. I shall never forget the moment I came back, conscious and alert. But the "disaster" was not over. Soon after I came out of the hospital, we found that my husband had a bad heart condition. He was compelled to give up his business and after a year he passed away. Then a few months later we discovered that my youngest son had tuberculosis, and I had to send him out West as soon as possible. I had to give up my apartment and go to work. I had never worked in the business world, but a friend who then owned a Travel Bureau made a place for me in it.

As I look back over the years that followed, it seems as though I were moving through a heavy, gray fog, in which fire flashed occasionally. Many messengers of the gods came into that little office. Some of them I saw only once; they came and went away, but always they spoke a word or two which seemed especially for me, though they never knew how I received their casual remarks. Others came definitely for the purpose of giving me important information regarding myself and the writings. A tall dark man came in one day and spent an hour talking to me like a brother. He spoke of the manuscript in my custody, which he seemed to know all about, and gave me much wise advice about what NOT to do with it. He told me to be patient and the way would open for the manuscript to be published, that I would really have little to do with it. I knew he was speaking truth, for I have never felt that I had anything to do with giving out this matter. I have never directed it. It directs me. But I am willing to obey orders—even to suffer, if suffering means growth for me and teaches me my part in the plan.

Another day a Buddhist monk came to see me. He had come from the Near East, he said, where he had been in a monastery for a long time and he was on his way to a monastery in Japan. He told me some amazing things which I do not feel at liberty to speak of, but for which I am deeply grateful. He said there were truths in the message given to me that had never been printed, but were given by word of mouth from master to student, and that it was significant of the change in the world that this fundamental truth was to be printed in a book where the layman could get it, if he wanted it. Then this man went away and I have never heard from him since.

So I came through these, humanly speaking, lonely years, and 1928 arrived. In February of that year, I received a positive order from *Sano Tarot* which said: "No time must be lost in preparing my words to be given to my people." This, after ten years of ordering me to be still.

It is probable that subconsciously I had been depending upon the fulfillment of the prophesy that two men would come to help me when it was time. Well, the men had not come and almost five years had passed. I hadn't the remotest idea what to do. I knew it had to be nicely typed before anything could be done. I had typed it myself on a decrepit machine and it looked like some strange, foreign language. A woman had offered to have it typed for $25.00. But that didn't help me because I didn't have $25.00.

I was sitting there in my room wondering what to do, when there was a knock on my door. I opened the door and there stood a lovely young woman who lived across the hall from me. I didn't know her name and she didn't know mine. She stood there like an angel, and asked: "What is it you do?"

The question was surprising, for how did she know I did anything? I answered her lightly: "You wouldn't be interested in what I do."

I thought she would see that I was not inclined to talk about my work. But no, she came right into my room and took a seat. "I'm going to stay until you tell me," she said.

"Well," I answered, "if you feel that way about it, I'll tell you."

So I told her this story and tried to interpret its meaning as it seemed to me.

We talked until after two o'clock in the morning and she, being of the new generation, understood it even better than I, who had set it down. Then I told her that the time had arrived when the message must move out to those who could respond to it. I told her that it must be nicely typed and asked her if $25.00 was cheap for the work of having it done. I will never forget the thrill of her answer: "Yes," she said, "that is cheap, but you are not going to pay it. I am going to do it myself, and for nothing. I am an authors' secretary. That is my business."

I was speechless! I knew that she was a part of the pattern being woven by the invisible forces who were directing the work.

She came in my room after that and brought her own typewriter and I read the writings to her while she typed them, which was the perfect way for it to have been done. The manuscript never left my hands. But the men who had been prophesied to help me had not come. I wondered, but I worked on. Then three days after my young friend finished typing the manuscript, a friend invited me to her home for tea one Sunday afternoon. I went, and there I met a man from Egypt. Of course, I wondered if he were the man who was prophesied as one who would assist me in some way regarding my writings. I remembered that *Sano Tarot* had said that he would hear of me through the publicity of the cross, so that was my key. If I found that this man knew about the cross, I would accept him as a friend of my work. So I kept still and awaited developments. He was a pleasant, formal man and said nothing which indicated that he had heard of the cross or me. I was a bit disappointed but it didn't seem to matter, and I dismissed him from my mind. Then later he said to me: "I have heard of you, Mrs. Fullwood."

My interest leaped, and I asked

him how and where he had heard of me.

"I know you as 'the lady with the cross'," he said.

I felt that he couldn't possibly realize what this meant to me. The invisible influences move so subtly. Our sensitive intelligence plays such a part in our spiritual understanding.

So dull and limited is the human mind that in spite of my inside information, I had a feeling of surprise. I asked him to tell me how he had heard of the cross and me.

His answer was awe-inspiring to me, who saw in it another strand woven by the invisible influences. The prophesy had been fulfilled in such a sane and natural way. Years before, a woman from my own Southland had been in New York. She heard about the cross and came to see me. She saw the cross and was greatly impressed with it and with the writings. Now, years later, she had been in Europe, had become acquainted with this man and had told him about me and the cross of light in my room and about the manuscript I had transcribed.

He asked me if he might read the manuscript and I gladly gave him my permission. So he came to see me and was deeply impressed with the beautiful rhythm of the writings. Then he said to me: "You have our teaching here. It has never been printed, but it is given by word of mouth from teacher to student." He said that the world had entered a time of crisis and that it was significant that fundamental truths were going to be given out so that the people who wanted them could get them. He said much the same thing that the Buddhist monk had said years before.

I asked him what he meant by "our teaching" and he told me that he was a

Coptic monk and had come from a monastery on the Arabian Desert. He told me many profound truths about world conditions in this day of the closing of a cycle of time, which corroborated what had been told me by invisible teachers. His coming was an event for which I was deeply grateful, and he contributed much that was needed at the time of the publishing of THE SONG OF SANO TAROT.

Three weeks afterward, the other man whose coming had been foretold, came from Paris. A mutual friend brought him to see me because he was a profound student of life and she thought he would be interested. He was. He was a literary man and knew just what to do with a strange book like this. He had a plan. He said the book must have a responsive audience waiting for it. He suggested that we send out announcements of the coming book to people who were awake to this sort of truth and see what would happen. He also suggested that we offer a small edition of 350 de Luxe books to be sold at five dollars each. I listened, but I doubted that it would work out as he hoped. When I expressed my uncertainty, he said, "That will be the supreme test. If this is what I think it is, you are in for a surprise." And sure enough I was. An interested and generous friend, Lillian Terry, gave me the money to have the circulars made and many people sent me lists of other friends who were definitely interested, and we sent the circulars out. Very soon the money began coming in, people buying the book in advance from the circular, and we soon had enough money to finance the publication.

One day I had a strange electrical experience. I had spent a whole day writing under tremendous concentration and that night I was very tired physically. I threw myself down on the couch and as I relaxed there was a flash accompanied by a loud report just over my head and the room was filled with a chemical odor which was both acid and sweetish. My first thought was that someone had thrown a bomb in the street. I sprang up and looked out of the window, but there was no sign of a disturbance of any kind. Then I went out into the hall to see if the odor was out there too, but it was not. It was all in my room. I called the man who had come from Paris and told him about the report and instantly he asked: "Was there an odor with it?" I tried to describe the odor to him and he seemed to understand it. He said that I was a highly charged electrical field and that such experiences must be taken as natural to me. But it has never occurred since.

The selection of a publisher was another interesting prophesy fulfilled. Over a period of years I had received a strange announcement from time to time, usually in the midst of my transcribing for *Sano Tarot*, saying: "The highpriest George is knocking at your door." I always got up and opened the door, but my visitor was invisible. I supposed that the title "'highpriest" indicated one of a religious nature, until a friend said, "Not necessarily, it could mean one in authority in any field." Later I asked this invisible messenger to be more explicit and tell me who the "highpriest George" was and why he was knocking at my door. I was told that he was one who stood high in the art of the bookmaking, and that I would find him "in the body of an English gentleman." This was not enough information to do anything about, so as usual, I waited.

Everything was ready now to find the right publisher. I had the name of a publisher who specialized in non-fiction books and one morning I made a sudden decision to go to see him and talk the matter over with him. He listened to me with sympathetic interest and said that they would publish the book. He explained to me that the business had been sold and I would have to see the present head of the house. He assured me that this man would be interested. He said he had been connected with one of the important standard publishing houses for many years until he had bought this business. He further explained that this man was not well and that he was there helping him because of his illness. "He is an Englishman," he went on casually, not knowing that my breath had stopped.

"An Englishman!" I exclaimed weakly, when my breath came back. Then I asked "What is his name?"

"George............................" he answered, unconscious of the tumult within me. There I had walked straight to an English publisher named George, and since he was "one in authority" I felt he must be the "highpriest George."

It was a whole week before I could go back to see this Englishman named George. I was so afraid he wouldn't come up to my expectations. But at last I went and found him indeed an English gentleman and an artist. He was interested in this type of knowledge and is responsible for the beautiful format in which THE SONG OF SANO TAROT is printed.

The book was almost ready for binding when disaster overtook this publishing house through the increased illness of the "highpriest George." He was forced to give up his business and it went into the hands of a receiver, my book along with the rest. Imagine my agony. I had accepted the subscribers' money for their books, and under this condition I didn't know whether I could ever deliver them. I did everything possible to get the book back into my own hands. The receiver told me that I could have it for two hundred dollars extra. Think of it! Where could I get two hundred dollars? It now seems to me that a host of demons had determined to prevent *Sano Tarot's* message from being given out. I didn't think of it that way then. I was too busy suffering. The men who had helped me had gone away, not expecting such a contingency. One of them had returned to Europe. I was alone for many months, never knowing which way to turn and when I did make a feeble move, I faced a blank wall. How often *Sano Tarot* said to me: "Patience yet a little while. My arms are around you. You could not fail me even if you would." But I was too desolate to be comforted.

Then suddenly the man who was holding the book decided that he would give it back to me with no extra payment. I think the gods had been working on him. The Macoy Publishing Company took the work over and the book was finished and delivered to its subscribers. The subscribers will never know how grateful I am for their patience during the delay.

I do not yet understand completely

the difficulty and delay. It may have been partly my lack of realization of the time element as expressed by *Sano Tarot* compared with my own limited conception of it, for long after the book was published, I found among my papers a communication from *Sano Tarot* which said: "My words will go forth to my people in the time singing to the riches of the Earth," which meant mid-summer, and here I had been trying to put it out in midwinter. Well, I couldn't do it. *Sano Tarot* had also told me: "The publication of my words is as fixed as your King's Insignia vibration through which it was given." I didn't know what the King's Insignia vibration was, nor do I know now, but I do know that whatever it is, I have dedicated it to the service of those who can use it. However, when the right time arrived for the publication of the book every obstacle disappeared and THE SONG OF SANO TAROT was born "in the time singing to the riches of the Earth."

During that year my son died in the West, and I thought life had finished for me. But somehow I kept on. Many letters of appreciation of the book came to me from people who had received illumination from it, while others said frankly that it was over their heads and they didn't know what it was all about. Many of the latter told me months and even years later that they didn't understand why they had not been able to "get" the message, since it had now all come clear to them after persistent reading and rereading. It was not long before the first edition was exhausted and the second edition was published.

Then another book, THE TOWER OF LIGHT, was given out from the Hermitage. This book consists of prophesies and promises given to me at intervals since 1917 and these prophesies are now being fulfilled in amazing ways. Then the third book was published, THE LIFE OF ONE WOMAN. This is a story of the recurrent birth of the soul. It was dictated by *Sano*

Tarot and the Timekeeper. *Sano Tarot* said of it: "This is the story of Uodeo, the Soul, as expressed in the eternal ebb and flow of the life of one woman."

THE SONG OF SANO TAROT is now in its third edition. It has gone all over the world. The writings move by their own power. I do not consider them mine. They find the people who are responsive to them. There is always an element of surprise to me in their movements. Some people whom I am certain will see their light, are just blank where the writings are concerned. While others, whom I least suspected would get anything from them, have received such illumination that they have been transformed from "the shadows of ignorance into the sunlight of spiritual understanding." The books have brought many people to me. Many of these bear names internationally known; authors, artists, musicians, actors, scientists and just plain people. I have not sought them. They have found me and have enriched my life with their interest and friendship.

During the years which have passed since I first became conscious of a higher dimension of life, I have been growing up to an understanding of it. Not that I have reached a full understanding by any means.

I will stop here, although it is not the end of the story which may be said to have no end. The communications continue, and my own realization of the spiritual purpose of life grows clearer as my comprehension of the fundamental law of equilibrium deepens.

I become more and more aware of the truth in the Timekeeper's message: "Man's great work is himself. His place of operation is wherever he finds himself, and his tools are the means at hand. There is no thing greater than another. Nothing high or low. Every experience is a stepping stone toward completion. The keynote of constructive living is BALANCE."

The nature of my clairvoyant experiences has been so changed since that sensitive period of years ago that today I look upon that first entry into the invisible world as the kindergarten of the later development.

At the time the gods first spoke to me I was not familiar with the theory of vibratory wave lengths which we hear so much about now in radio operation, but this theory serves as a splendid example of what might be the mode of procedure employed by the invisible forces which have taught and used me. I feel that there is a group of beings gathered about a microphone, as it were, in the Hermitage Tower (The Sun) and I sense, or hear with intuitive hearing, one of them speaking to me, and I also hear them talking to each other of me as a "channel." I have a distinct impression that they are not interested in me as a personality. I am simply something to be used and I am willing to be used according to my capacity and am grateful for any service required of me.

If I were a man I would probably be a preacher, and my little flock would believe me when I told them I had been in the sun and discovered that it was not hot there, and that it is the dwelling place of spiritual beings; and that I had been in the center of the Earth and found what seemed to me to be another sun there; and that sometimes I am with beings of enormous size and great beauty. I have been in monasteries in far away places. I have received information of which I cannot speak, and prophesies which have already come true, as well as many yet to be fulfilled.

I suppose all this will sound strange to many, and to others—though they may never have heard of such things before—

it will be real. To me it is as natural as breathing.

As I have said before, I am a very practical person. Abstract theories do not interest me. I like things that work, and after years of experiencing and observing in others the constructive, uplifting and regenerative power of this spiritual Force operating under the symbol *Sano Tarot,* I can truly say that it works.

Finis

CPSIA information can be obtained
at www.ICGtesting.com
Printed in the USA
LVHW081559040219
606316LV00038B/1698/P